UN
APOLOGETICALLY
UNJADED
what loving him taught me about myself

Annata. R

RIVERS PUBLISHING © 2022

ALL RIGHTS RESERVED

Dedicated to all the women
with a story inside of them…

tell it.

It is said that life lessons will keep repeating themselves until they are learned.
I've learned a lot of lessons, and my hope is that through my story, maybe I can save you from going down the path that I did, or at least inspire you to get off that path if you're already on it.

I hope that my story sheds a bright light on why it's so important to do our inner work, confront our shadows, gain self-awareness, and be honest with ourselves no matter how much the truth we come face to face with hurts. The truth is the only thing that can set us free, after all.

When we don't know the true meaning of love, or we're desperate to be loved we often end up in situations with people we never thought we would, wrapped up in a thick fog of shame and embarrassment which can leave us feeling isolated. It's important to know, however, we actually aren't ever alone in anything we go through.

Mind your business

"One thing about the universe, it will test you to see just how serious you are about your growth."

How many sentences have you started with, "There I was, minding my business..."

Well, there I was, minding my business when he came out of nowhere. I had spent the last year doing the most. My marriage was over, and I was officially separated but I felt like I had missed out on so much for so many years that it was time to make up for it. I was going out, dating, partying, travelling. I was painting the town whatever colors I wanted, having the time of my life. Eventually though, I ran out of steam and took a time-out to focus more on myself, my kids, my health, and my jobs. I was in what I like to call, "my Zen mode" which was a really good place for me to be in. I definitely wasn't looking for any man when he approached me, and the moment he did I knew he was a bad idea. Why?
Because he was a whole married man, and a janitor in the library I was working in part-time.

"*How you get them is how you lose them*" I heard the voices of my elders echo throughout my mind. My plan was to listen to those voices. As a matter of

fact, I wasted no time in telling him that I was not interested in the slightest. I even went as far as to tell him that I was completely over men for the moment and that niggas were lame.
You know what he did? Laughed.
A soft, sexy, laid-back laugh escaped his lips right before he parted them to respond, "I'm different though."

My plan was to listen to the voices of my elders echoing throughout my mind, but there was something about him that made me shush them instead.

Oh, you're a charmer, charmer

"Charm is more valuable than beauty because you can resist beauty, but you can't resist charm."

A man with charm is a very dangerous thing.
I don't think I had ever met anyone as brazen as him in my life. There's a thin line between confident and cocky, I just wasn't sure which one he was.
At first glance there was nothing really special about him. I mean, he wasn't the "tall, dark and handsome" type, if you know what I mean.
He was regular.
Regular height, regular build, regular medium skin tone. He was unshaven and his hair was a braided mess, but he had a smile that would stop any woman in her tracks. The way his dimples graced his cheeks in perfect harmony with each other while revealing a set of pearly white teeth—that's what drew me in.
The way he looked at me was what pulled me in a little closer. It was as though he saw straight into and through me. He made me blush in ways that sent electric sparks throughout my entire body, and I liked it. What kept me hooked was his way with words. He was a smooth talker, the perfect salesman, so naturally I believed him when he said that his marriage was over and he was moving out

of the home they shared, into his own place. I knew the process of separation, the steps needed to move forward with a divorce, and how tedious that in between time could be far too well, as I too was in the middle of my own separation.
Thinking back on it, I probably didn't need much convincing when he asked me to give him a chance. I wasn't thinking about anyone except myself—what I wanted, what I needed, how I felt. I didn't know then all that I know about self-love now, and maybe if I had I would have never entertained him, let alone immerse myself in him.
The more we talked, the more deeply we connected. We were both completely at ease with each other. There were no filters, no judgements.
We were both free to be ourselves.
The connection and chemistry were an exciting bonus. Kissing him felt so familiar, as though our lips had once lost each other and now found their way back home. The first time I kissed him, I knew that I wasn't going to be able to stop.
It was like an addiction.
We couldn't get enough of each other, and the spontaneity made it feel all the more exhilarating. From that first kiss to the first time we explored each others' bodies, a fire ignited inside of me that I couldn't put out... that I didn't want to put out.
A fire that would burn only for him.
He'd steal me away on lunch breaks and take me to hotels. We'd meet in the bathroom, in the basement

between the bookcases, in my office, in the car in the parking lot, in dressing rooms at the mall and bathrooms at the restaurant.

We would ravish each other anywhere, everywhere, it didn't matter. I'd never felt so alive before.

The sex was unmatched.

It made me wonder what I'd been doing all the years prior. I'd often ask him, "What do you want from me?" His answer was always the same.

In a low, seductive voice, he would respond, *"Your soul..."*

Love and Lust

Love is defined as an intense feeling of deep affection. Lust is defined as very strong sexual desire.

When he told me that he loved me I believed him. Something inside of me felt it.
He asked if I felt the same way about him and I was honest when I told him I wasn't sure. I was definitely feeling something, but was it love?
Is obsession part of love?
Is addiction part of love?
He was all I thought about and wanted all the time. Lust can feel a lot like love when you're addicted to someone.
Ultimately, I decided for myself that it *was* love. I honestly didn't think I would feel love again because I was so let down by it in the past, but here I was, and I felt so alive.
When he finally moved out of his wife's house, of course I was happy. He was free which meant *we* were finally able to be free together.
I'd spend nights at his place, and he'd spend nights at mine. It felt great laying on his chest and falling asleep, him playing with my hair, me playing with his, the random forehead kisses, the physical closeness—I loved it all. I loved him and he loved me, at least, that was the story I told myself.

We never talked about the future or if we even had one. When we were together it was like nothing else in the world existed, or even mattered. It was just the two of us. No real thought process, no end game, no future. Just us living in the moment.

You know what they say though…
it's all fun and games until someone loses an eye.

July 19th, 2019

Dear Punkin',

I love you so much and I'm so sorry.
Sorry for the doubt that you felt even though I tried my best to mask it.
Sorry for the stress that I probably transferred onto you.
Sorry that I couldn't save you.
I tried.
I begged and pleaded with God to keep you, but He said no, and I know that He knows best.
This hurts so bad, but this world just wasn't ready for you my sweet, sweet, Angel baby. I'm so sorry.

Love Always,
Your Mom

When I first found out that I was pregnant, I was very nervous and rightly so. We were living such a carefree life, then all of a sudden, face to face with something serious.

His excitement about the news put me at ease though. He was over the moon, and had already claimed the fetus in my belly to be a girl and gave her a name. Sadly, it was all short lived.

I'd never lost a baby before. I felt like my body was betraying me.

"Why is this happening? Is it my fault? Did I do something wrong?"

When I delivered him the news, he made his disappointment known, then retreated into a shell. We didn't really speak about it much after that, but I began reflecting deeply on my own.

Were we not supposed to have a baby together?

Dodged that bullet

There's an old saying that my mom would always recite, *"You play with the pups, and you get bitten by the fleas."*

The Universe will always give you an out, but it's up to you to take it.
Sometimes when I think about my miscarriage I feel like it was my out.
Maybe God was trying to tell me something.
Maybe I wasn't supposed to be attached to this man for the rest of my life.
Maybe I dodged a bullet.
Dodging a bullet sounds like it should be such a relief, right? But just imagine dodging a bullet only to go back and play with the gun.

Okay, what just happened?

And just like that everything changed.
They say that when you look at someone through rose colored glasses, the red flags just look like… flags.

I remember the day so distinctly, like it was yesterday.
I was in my office at the library, and we were texting as usual. He was getting ready to finish his shift and was going to stop by so he could see, touch, and feel me before he left.
Of course I was excited.
Butterflies swarmed my tummy as I smiled at the phone. Within seconds after the last message, there he was in front of me, his dimples so pronounced. He licked his lips and moved toward me after closing my office door.
"Hey," was all he managed to say before his lips were on mine, one hand grabbing my hair, the other between my thighs. The fire inside of me was rising from my feet to my throat, and I welcomed it. As I unbuttoned his pants and was about to release the zipper, the phone on my desk started ringing.
I hesitated to answer but the ring was so persistent that I picked up. My manager was on the other end asking for help with an important project.

"We'll finish this later," he whispered in my ear as he ran his thumb across my cheek and gently kissed me goodbye.
I melted as I watched him leave, wishing he didn't have to, then sighed as I searched my computer for the file my manager needed.
I buttoned my top two buttons, fixed my hair in place, then made my way to fulfill my work task.
I was smiling as I walked into my managers office. I handed her the file, then randomly peered out her window as she reviewed it. My heart skipped a beat when I saw the man who I almost made passionate love to on my desk moments earlier, standing on the street. I touched my pocket for my phone to text him, but realized that I'd forgotten it on my desk.
A feeling of pure bliss washed over me as I looked at him standing there. Flashbacks of us just moments ago invaded my mind and I wanted to be in his arms again where I felt the best.
In a split second, the blissful feeling was replaced with a gut-wrenching pain as my heart dropped, like a glass vase falling to the floor and shattering into a million pieces.

I stared in disbelief as a small red Toyota pulled up directly in front of him, and a woman hopped out of the driver seat. She was shorter than him and very fair in complexion. Her hair was tied with a head tie, and the clothes she wore were baggy. She kissed him on the cheek then walked over to the passenger side as he replaced her in the driver's seat, and they drove off.

What. The. Fuck?

My mind began to race.
The passionate fire that had I just felt turned quickly into a paralyzing burn.
What just happened? Who was she?
I knew it wasn't his wife because even though I hadn't ever seen her before, I knew her car was a black BMW and not a red Toyota. I was so confused and immediately felt sick to my stomach.
I asked my manager if all was good with the files. After thumbing through them a little more, she gave me a satisfactory nod, which I return with a fake smile, then turned on my heels and made my way back to my office. I contemplated on what I was going to do or say to the man who was supposed to be *my* lover.
Returning to my office I picked up my phone and opened our thread. I read the last message where he said that he wanted me so bad, and I immediately felt like it was all calculated, like he knew that he was going to be picked up and wanted to make sure that I was in my office and stayed there.

I typed, "Nice red car you got into."

Almost immediately his response came in.
"What are you talking about?"

"Don't even bother lying. I saw you and I saw her."
I was tempted to call but there was a knot in my throat.
"So, what? You don't trust me now? Look, I can't do this with you right now, okay? I'll talk to you later."
His message was cold. I didn't deserve that.
"Don't even bother. There isn't anything to talk about. I should have left you alone a long time ago."

I threw my phone onto the desk and couldn't hold back the tears. I felt so stupid.
There I was, high as a kite one minute, then laid out flat the next. I left work that afternoon and decided that I would spend the weekend at my friend's house. I didn't want to be at home, but I didn't want to be alone, either.
That night he called but I didn't answer. The next day he called and texted—I still didn't answer. This was the first time since we met that I didn't speak to him at all. Him being married was one thing. Yes, I knew it was wrong, but knowing they were separated and knowing (or thinking I knew) that it was a terrible marriage, based on what he had said so many times, I justified my being with him. I understood I was technically the other woman, I knew I had signed up for *that*.
But who was this *other* woman? How? Why? Where did she come from? How long had she been around? *This* was too much.

The weekend passed and we didn't speak although I wanted to talk to him and get my questions answered. I wrestled with the idea of calling in sick that Monday but decided against it, I still needed to make my money.

I wasn't in my office for more than five minutes when he barged into the room and shut the door behind him.

"Are you crazy? You can't do that!" I protested.

He grabbed my face and kissed me hard, but I shut my lips and didn't kiss him back. He shoved his hand down my pants and pressed his mouth against my ear as he gripped me with his hand, "Don't ever ignore me when you see me calling you. You're mine until the day I die, do you understand? You're not going anywhere."

He removed his hand from between my legs, squeezed my cheeks, then turned and walked away. My heart was beating out of my chest and also in my pants.

What just happened?

I don't think I had ever felt a rush like that in my entire life. Make no mistake though, I wasn't naive enough to ignore the fact that it was also toxic as fuck.

He called me within minutes of leaving my office and I answered like it was a regular day. He briefly addressed the subject of the woman in the red Toyota because I'm guessing he knew it would come up eventually. I had so many questions but there was almost no point in asking them. He got ahead of the problem by reassuring me that I had nothing to worry about with her, and all that mattered was how he felt about me, how we felt about each other. Our chemistry was rare, our connection was real, and he wasn't letting that go.

I was in such a weird place because it all felt like a high to me. I felt desired and wanted in the worst way. By the time he was done smoothing me over with his words, I didn't even remember that there was a whole other woman in the picture. I honestly didn't care. She didn't matter because he still wanted me, and to me… that's all that mattered.

It's whatever

You have an intuition for a reason... use it.

At this point, *nothing* was tying us together except great sex. We could have literally gone our separate ways, but we didn't. Between losing the baby and finding out about the other woman, my enthusiasm for him had somewhat subsided. We still loved each other, and he was adamant about not letting me go. I on the other hand wished he *would* let me go.
Why didn't I just end it myself?
Self-love had not yet entered the chat.
The spark was still there, our sex was still amazing and surprisingly somewhat consistent. Surprisingly because I couldn't understand where was he finding the time for the other woman *and* me? But I just didn't see him in the same light I once did—how could I?
Looking back now, I think the bubble of carelessness that we lived in had deflated, leaving me face to face with the real consequences of our actions, and face to face with who he really was. Now I was asking myself if there was anything beyond the sex. Lust and love are not the same thing, and I was learning this lesson the hard way. I started thinking about my future and if he fit in it. I knew that I wasn't ready to bring a man around my kids. At the same time, I also knew there was

something about him that I didn't want to let go of, even though my intuition kept screaming at me to. It was that "potential" so many of us women put above reality. The fantasy of who we believe a man can become.
I should have let him go because of who he was and what he was showing me, but I didn't. I chose to hold on to who he had the potential to be, the man I believed he could become. The man that he promised he would become.
And that's exactly how I kept betraying myself.

Hindsight is always twenty-twenty. Right?

About last night...

Sometimes we get so caught up in the glitz and glamour, we forget it's the simple things in life that usually mean the most.

It was his birthday.
I had no intentions of seeing him let alone spending it with him, but I had gotten him a small gift.
He was an avid cognac drinker so when I saw an ad for a personalized Hennessy label, I got him a bottle with his name on it and left it with his friend so he could pick it up whenever he had the time.
Later that night he called to thank me and asked if I wanted to come hang out with him for his birthday, which I wasn't expecting at all because we hadn't spoken about any plans, but I agreed.
His one request—which was the only request he ever made whenever we went out—was for me not to wear any panties. It reminded me of that bubble we used to be in, and how exciting him would make my own body parts tingle.
The weather that evening was perfect for the outfit I chose. I wore a medium wash, blue denim dress that hit right at mid-thigh, with a pair of tall cognac-colored boots. I styled my hair in a low bun with a side part, put a pair of gold hoops in my ears, then completed my look with a long leather jacket.

It's always about the simplicity.

I met him at his boy's house.
All three of us hung out for a little bit, had some drinks, and cracked some jokes while music played at just the right level in the background. After about an hour, his boy left us alone to have some privacy. There was something about the vibes that night, I can't quite put my finger on it, but not only did it end up being one of our best nights together, but also one of the best dates I had ever had. Nothing fancy...just *us*.
We laughed, talked, dance, sang, kissed and fucked on every surface of that area.
The stairs, the floor, the wall, but it was the chair that had me floating. Chair sex was usually him sitting and me straddling him either from the front or the back, but this time it was different. This time it was nothing I had ever experienced before.
He made me climb onto the chair facing backwards and I was in perfect alignment for him to enter me with ease and boy did he numerously. I definitely lost count of how many times I orgasmed.
"Is this my birthday or yours?" I whispered in his ear as I could feel him still throbbing inside of me. The passion between us that night was intoxicating, and felt like old times, like we were back in our fantasy bubble without a care in the world and neither of us wanted to leave it. Eventually, we left his boys house and decided to continue our night in a cozy, seductively lit lounge that was nearby.

We nestled close to each other while he kept his hand between my legs. I kept wishing we could just freeze time. We stayed until closing, then I drove him back to his place and parked up.

It was evident that neither of us wanted the night to come to a close, because we ended up staying in the car talking about life, love, us…and everything in between. And of course, it wouldn't be us if we didn't slide into the back seat where I could straddle him one last time. I didn't think I had any energy left in me to be able to orgasm again, but as we were moving in perfect sync, with the final thrust came the final release.

It felt good to escape the reality of our situation if just for one night, and what an epic night it was.

It's a boy

Once we become parents, we have to remember that the decisions we make no longer just affect us, they affect our children, too.

Neither of us were thinking or being careful so it was bound to happen, but deep down, we both wanted it.

I was pregnant again

It's funny (not really though) because based on his wife and the other, *other* woman's calculations, the running joke is that it happened on that epic birthday night. Truth be told, and confirmed by medical professionals, conception had already taken place prior to that night.

This time it was my birthday, and my best friend was planning my party and gender reveal, so she put him in charge of getting me away from the house for the weekend. We rented a hotel on Long Island, then he made reservations at one of my favorite restaurants. He even borrowed his friend's Mercedes Benz for the evening so he could take me to dinner in style. I felt so fancy.

It had been a while since we'd gone out, and it felt nice to get dressed up and see him dressed up for me. The baby bump was already showing, and he couldn't stop rubbing, and talking to it. From the beginning he thought it was a girl. He said that God only gave men like him girls because of how poorly they treated women. The logic being, "Now you will see that the women you treated poorly were daughters of people, too." Some sort of twisted logic, but it proved that he was definitely aware of his shit.

Dinner was great.
We talked and laughed as though we were the only two people in the world, as usual. He was pleasantly surprised to learn that even in my pregnant state, I still managed to keep our tradition of not wearing panties when we went out. Needless to say, his hands were very warm between my thighs as we drove throughout the city. After we got back to the hotel and made love, we showered together then crawled back into the bed where he held me in his arms. There was an energy about him while we laid there, one that I couldn't quite put my finger on. My head on his chest, I peered up at him to see if I could read his face. He smiled warmly at me, but the look in his eyes told me that there was something he wanted to say. I smiled back at him, hoping he would take it as an invite to reveal whatever was on his heart, but he didn't. Instead, he just pulled me closer to him as he took a deep breath, inhaling the scent of my freshly washed hair. I wanted to ask him if he was okay, but I didn't. Whatever it was, he didn't want to talk about it, and

as I laid in his arms drifting off to sleep, I decided that was fine by me.

The next day was my birthday and the big gender reveal. It was intimate and exciting.

We were finally going to find out what we were having. This was also the first time my mother and kids would be meeting the mystery man behind the baby bump.

They all stood around as my friend presented me with the large, beautifully wrapped box. I opened it and expected for either blue or pink balloons to pop out, but was met with neither. Instead, the box contained white balloons, confetti, a huge bottle of chocolate syrup and an old gaming system.

"What the..." I started, but before I could finish, she handed me a small white gift bag with blue and pink tissue paper peeking out from the top. My heart raced as I removed the paper to discover a grey tuxedo romper with the cutest bowtie attached. We were having a boy.

I was emotional as I looked over to him, "There you go! It's a boy!"

I watched the state of shock flash across his face, before he smiled wide and hugged me. After all, he *had* convinced himself we were going to have a girl.

"I love you," he whispered in my ear, and my heart melted.

"I love you more," I whispered back.

...

The thing I felt like he had on his heart that night at the hotel finally came to light.

He was moving back home with his wife.

Did I miss something?

He claimed that he was losing his place and had no choice, but I wasn't buying it. If you want something bad enough, you will fight for it, and in this case, the fight would be for freedom.

I got the overwhelming sense he wanted to make it work with his wife, and when I told him that, he got upset and reiterated that he "had no choice."

Everything is a choice.

Why wasn't I a choice?

Before I could ask he told me that he loved me and admired my strength as a woman and mother, however, he saw the struggles I faced being a single mother with no support. He wanted to be the one who could support me, not become a burden adding to my already full plate. He went on to explain that he wasn't in a position to help me because he couldn't even help himself.

I'd often tell him that I believed in him more than he believed in himself. He'd portray the tough guy exterior, but deep down I saw the lost puppy in him. On his last night at his place, he asked me to spend it with him. I was reluctant at first, but he insisted.

I should have trusted my intuition.

When I got there things were okay, but as the evening progressed he became distracted and jumpy. We had sex but it was different. There was no passion or intimacy. Little did I know that it would also be the last time that we'd have sex for the duration of my pregnancy.

He moved back to his home with his wife and was miserable. I'm not sure what he expected; if it was bad when he left and no effort was made to improve the situation, then chances were he was walking into a worse situation with anger and resentment added to the mix.

He had to bite the bullet and break the news of the pregnancy to her. Obviously she didn't take it well, why would she? He used the fact that he was out of the house at the time to his advantage and as an explaination for his indiscretion.

It would be that initial confession to his wife that would prompt even more confessions…

Baby mama drama

"Drama doesn't walk into your life. Either you create it, invite it, or associate with it." – Brooke Hampton

I remember the day so well.
It was a Saturday afternoon and he Facetimed me from work.
"What's the one thing I could do that would make you stop loving me?" He asked.
"What are you talking about?" I responded.
Silence.
"HELLO?" I shouted.
My emotions were already running wild thanks to the pregnancy hormones. I was nervous, annoyed, sad, anxious, confused and angry all at the same time.

"Someone else is pregnant for me," he finally let out.

My heart. Oh my God my heart.
I felt it sink into the pits of my stomach as my mind began to race. I wanted to say something, but the immediate dryness of my throat prevented me so instead I let him talk. He had always said that I was his lover and best friend because he could tell me anything and knew I wouldn't judge him, so he

began sharing details with me that I didn't care to hear at that moment.
He told me how they met, that they'd only slept together twice, and that she wanted to keep the baby because she wanted to keep *him*. He told her he didn't want the baby, couldn't afford the baby, was back home with his wife, *and* already had a baby on the way. While I heard everything he said, his voice sounded distant to me, almost as though he was speaking under water because all that kept replaying in my mind was my own voice asking, "*Another woman… pregnant?*"

I felt defeated at this point.
How many more bombs could I take from him? There was always a big part of me that felt like our relationship was special, and hearing all this made me feel reduced to just another girl who got pregnant while he was living on his own. When he finally realized I wasn't giving him the reaction he expected, he asked me what I was thinking.
"It has to be exhausting being you," I began.
"All the shit you got going on in your life and you manage to get another woman pregnant…it's like you live for the drama."
Anytime a topic was heavy, and he didn't want to talk about it anymore, his response would always be a deep sigh. This time was no different.

All I could do was shake my head. I mean, what else was I supposed to say?
There I was, six months pregnant with his baby, trying to recover from the blow of him moving back in with his wife and now this?

This was all too much, and I was tired…at least, that's the story I told myself.

Side Chick to the Side Chick

If you start a relationship being the other woman, you will never be the only woman.

Time was passing, our son was due soon, and the way we carried on, you would think the conversation about the other woman being pregnant never happened.
I was living in delusion, I know that now.
I kept wanting to save him from himself.
Trust me I know how that sounds, but that's the truth. Again, if I knew then what I know now about self-love, this story would be completely different.
Ready for another bomb? I definitely wasn't.

He finally made the decision to move out of his wife's house, for good this time, but instead of getting his own place, he was going to move in with the woman who owned the red Toyota. Yes the same woman he told me I didn't have anything to worry about all those months ago. Here she was now stepping into her promotion.
"Homegirl" is what he now called her.

I was speechless. I didn't know what to make of it, but honestly, what could I make of it? It's like I had nothing left in me at that point and definitely

running out of emotions to feel. It happened, it was happening, and it had obviously *been* happening.
I don't have any right to make any assumptions or even speak on this woman because I don't know her and it's not my place. I jokingly referred to her as the MVP, because in actuality, that's exactly what she was to him.
She gave him a roof over his head, a car to drive, phones, clothes and whatever else he needed. She saved him. She did the most for him, so he valued her the most i.e., she was the MVP. I really don't blame him, I mean women do it all the time don't they? Go for the guy with the most money? The most security and stability.
Maybe she didn't mind being the "homegirl" because while he might still be out there messing around, he went home to her. We all put up with what we choose to put up with, I for sure am not one to judge because as you've read thus far I've put up with quite a bit as well. Maybe in her eyes, him coming home to her made it all worth it. Or like myself him "loving" her made it all worth it. Who knows? She's the only one that can answer that question. He needed her and she knew it and she was there for him. She got him in a way that nobody else did, vulnerable. The way he spoke about her I knew that she wasn't going anywhere. She was determined to be his everything. Exactly what his wife and anyone else who came before her weren't.

She made sure she was there for him in every possible way so there would be no room for error. Sure she had her slip ups here and there like checking his phone and tracking her car but those can probably be chalked up to warranted insecurities. Here she was trying so hard and doing everything possible, everything "right", so why was it still not enough? Why was he still doing whatever he wanted?

I know that everything I say will sound like it's coming from a place of bitterness or jealousy, but the truth is I don't envy her because she's not in a better position than I am. I'm not in a better position than she is. The simple fact is that in situations like these there are no winners, not even him. She'll never fully have him, I'll never fully have him, nobody will, and he will never have peace. How can he? With all of these women that he's juggling.

All of the women involved in his web are guilty of one thing...*loving him.* As strange as it sounds, we probably all actually believed that he loved us back. We all have choices in life, he was mine, but she was his. He chose her because she was the best choice for him—plain and simple.
I was never mad at him for choosing her. I was mad because he chose her but still wouldn't let me go. False hope can sometimes hurt more than lies...that belief that we could actually be something.

First I was the side chick to his wife, and obviously so was the woman in the red Toyota. Now here I was the side chick to her. So I became the side chick to the side chick, but how can I really complain when I chose to be a part of the chaos, confusion, and intentional crossroads.
Those of us who willingly entangled ourselves in his web can deny it all we want, but deep down we probably all wanted to be the one he chose in the end. However, we all need to realize that when it comes to a man like him, there will never be "the one"…there will only be one of many.

Hard pills to swallow

What am I doing?

I'm a beautiful, intelligent woman with a heart of gold and a soul that gives the purest of love.

Why on earth did I continue to play so small, water myself down and settle? Why was he my choice when it was crystal clear that I wasn't his? Why did I continue sleeping with him? Who was benefiting? After he took his shower to wash off any remnants of me, put his clothes back on and leave me laying there in my empty bed to go back to the house and bed that he shared with her. *She was his choice.* How did that feel every single time? He said he loved me, but did he value me? Did he respect me? Was that really love? More importantly, was it the type of love that I wanted or needed?

My prince is here

"For I know the plans I have for you" declares the Lord, "plans to prosper you and not to harm you, plans to give you hope and a future" - Jeremiah 29:11

This pregnancy was very different compared to my other ones.

My other pregnancies I was comfortable, pampered and catered to. I also worked from home so that was a big plus. This pregnancy however, I was waking up every morning and commuting into work, five days a week, right up until the week before I gave birth. My body was tired. My hormones were playing tricks on my sugar levels, so I had extra appointments for close monitoring. Then there was the fact that he wasn't there for me, and I wasn't used to that. The father of my other children never left my side during my pregnancies.

He did offer to go with me to *one* of my earlier appointments but due to the pandemic, only the mom was allowed at the appointments. I didn't expect him to wait on me hand and foot or be with me every single day, but I did think that he'd be more present than he was.

By the grace of God and the support of my friends and family I made it through, and so did my baby.

My best friend was with me for the delivery. Due to the pandemic, the rules were specific and strictly enforced. One person was allowed in the room during delivery, and they were not allowed to leave. Once they left the hospital, they wouldn't be able to return. I remember his words when I explained that to him.

"You know why I won't be able to make it, right?"

A part of me hoped that he would find a way to make it to his own son's birth, but of course he "wouldn't be able to be there", he didn't want to *upset* his "homegirl" by running off in the middle of the night to wait for his baby to be born. Once again his choice was clear as day.

My son was born and that too was a different experience than my other births. Minutes after he came out, the nurse noticed that his breathing was very short and rapid, so they immediately took him to the NICU. I was scared out of my mind.

I messaged him to let him know his son was here along with what was going on, and he ended up coming to visit us with food and snacks for me the next day.

I mean... thanks?

Due to my IV, I still hadn't seen my son since the nurses took him, so my now baby daddy went to the

NICU to spend some time with him. When he came back and said that he looked good, it calmed me a little bit. He stayed a while, we talked mostly about the baby, then he left.
That night after the IV provided its last drops I was finally allowed to go see my baby. I couldn't hold him, but I could touch him inside of his little glass house. My baby daddy Facetimed me while I was there, and made it feel like we both were with him.

The following day I was discharged.
My heart was heavy because I already knew that my son wouldn't be coming home with me. Baby daddy came to pick me up and finished signing all of the paperwork for our son's birth certificate, then we took turns seeing him before leaving the hospital.
I was silent for most of the car ride home. He kept reassuring me that everything was going to be okay, but I was barely listening. Honestly, this entire experience was traumatizing. From being alone most of my pregnancy, to him moving back in with his wife, to finding out another woman was pregnant, to him moving out of his wife's house and in with a whole other women, to him not even being at the birth of his own son, to our baby being in the NICU… I was spent.

He dropped me off at home where I crawled into my bed and cried myself to sleep. I remember praying that I would wake up and everything would be okay, that my baby would be in my arms, and his father would be right there by our side.

If only…

A mother's job is never done

Agatha Christie once said, "A mother's love for her child is like nothing else in the world."

The next morning, I was awakened by a panicked phone call from the hospital, "You need to come in *right now*."

I was delirious and didn't know what to do or think. I washed my face, threw on some clothes and got an Uber because there was no way I could drive in my state. When I got to the NICU, my baby was surrounded by at least ten doctors, and my heart raced. As I approached the scene, I noticed my sweet little boy had a lot more tubes in him. My heart immediately sank. I felt like he was in pain, and I couldn't do anything to help him.
The doctors explained that he had to be transferred to a better equipped hospital because the services they were trying to provide him at the moment were not improving his health. They needed me to come immediately to authorize the transfer, which of course I did. Within the next few minutes, they were loading him into the back of an ambulance, and I was hopping into the front seat of a Supervisor Ambulance car to follow closely behind. The sounds, the speed, the red lights and my fast-beating heart felt surreal.

When we got to the transfer hospital in the city, I had to wait outside in the lobby so they could get him set up. I watched in fright and frustration as the hours went by. It would be five hours before I was allowed to see him. I eventually learned that every time they would stabilize him, he would keep taking a turn for the worst. Before they could let me see him, they needed him to be consistently stable.

By the grace of God, they were finally able to get him to stay stable and I was allowed to enter his room. I stood over him, my eyes taking in all of the tubes everywhere. I was in awe at the little fighter he was. Before he came in this world, baby daddy and I had toyed with the name Jeremiah, meaning "Appointed by God". I decided right there and then that Jeremiah would be my son's name.

Later in the night, baby daddy came to pick me up. He went in to talk with the doctors, see his son, then we left.

I was happy he was there. I was so exhausted, so drained, and I needed the support, but true to his patterns that support was short lived.
He stopped, grabbed me some food, and once we arrived at my place, he reassured me again that everything would be okay, then left.
Jeremiah stayed in the hospital for the following six days and got stronger and stronger. Every single one of those days I made the trek to the city, and

cherished every minute with him. The first time I got to hold him again since the day I pushed him out was so emotional. I got to breastfeed him, bond with him…talk to him and just hold him close to me.

Baby daddy never came back to visit.
It was always one excuse after the next, and at that point, not only did I not expect anything more from him, but I also genuinely didn't have time or the emotional space to care. I was focused on what really mattered—Jeremiah.

…

Euphoria

noun

A feeling or state of intense excitement and happiness

Insanity

noun

Doing the same thing over and over expecting a different result.

Stupidity

noun

A behavior that shows a lack of good sense or judgement.

Yeah, all three of the words are best to describe what I did next.
The birth of our son could have been a new beginning for the both of us in simple co-parenting roles. I know I didn't have to go back down the rabbit hole with him, but I did.
Two weeks after giving birth and one week after the baby came home from the hospital… it happened. One kiss was all it took, it was all it ever took, and that kiss felt like the first time all over again.

All of the other women, him not being there for his own son, him not being there for me—all of it went out the window as soon as he laid his lips on mine. Instead of choosing self-respect and self-love, instead of choosing not to let him have his way with me, I choose the opposite.

Once again, I chose the euphoria, insanity and stupidity for myself.
Why?

Rumor has it

What happens in dark always comes to light.

He'd come by to visit us, we'd have our little time together, then he'd go home… back to his woman. That isn't what I wanted.
I wanted to be able to watch our son fall asleep on his father's chest, and wake in the morning to him, but none of that would ever happen.
All I could get from him was what he was willing to give, so that's what I settled for… crumbs.
He would say that it wouldn't always be this way, that he was doing what he had to do so he could get his shit together so that he could do better for me and for us.
I continued to settle for those crumbs though, because I wanted to believe him, and as crazy as I know it sounds, I still had hope for us.

My maternity leave was up, and it was time for me to return to my jobs. He no longer worked as a janitor at the library as he had moved on to a better paying job elsewhere right before our son was born. One day while using the restroom at work, I heard two women talking and recognized their voices as the cashiers from our mini food court area. I had finished handling my business, but lingered inside the stall for a while longer listening to their conversation. One of them was crying as she explained her situation to the other.

Apparently, she found out that she was pregnant not too long before, but the father of the baby was not supportive at all.

"I just feel so alone," she sobbed.

I was immediately triggered because I could definitely relate to the feeling.

The other woman was showing her compassion, but also sharing her opinion.

"I don't even know why you ever messed with that stupid, low life janitor to begin with…"

She said his name aloud, and my stomach damn near sank into the toilet bowl.

Who?

I continued listening as my heart felt like it wanted to force itself out of my chest. The more details they spoke, the more they confirmed that yes, they were indeed talking about my and now baby daddy.

After they left, I slowly made my way out of the bathroom. I was sick to my stomach, my legs were shaking, my hands were shaking...damn.

Another one?

I immediately called him to confront him about what I had just overheard.

At first he acted dumb, but then finally said,

"I told her to stop saying that I'm the father because who knows if it's really mine."

What the fuck?

That was it. That was his explanation.

There was a moment of pause on the line. I didn't know what to say. I had a thousand feelings at once, but the three feelings that I felt pulsating through my veins the most were, deep sadness, rage, and embarrassment.
Really? Another one?
How was this happening again?
And this time, right in my face?
Another woman pregnant.
Another woman pregnant who worked in the *same damn building* as I did and as he used to.
How much more could my heart take?
I don't know which was hurting me more, the woman who worked in my building being pregnant, or him literally offering *zero* type of remorse.

What was I supposed to say to this? I was always left speechless because none of it felt like real life...but it was.
I ended the call without saying another word.

Inevitable

You don't need to be a psychic to see certain things coming.

I should have left him alone, right?
I mean, you're reading this story and you're thinking to yourself, "Okay, this time she's *for sure* done with him, right?"
They say every woman's "enough is enough" moment is different.
Apparently, I was a glutton for punishment i.e his bullshit.
I didn't want to let him go.
I felt like I *couldn't* let him go.
I still wanted to believe things would change, that he would come around, that he would one day soon, somehow, look at all we'd been through and decide this is where he wanted to be forever.
In hindsight, was it really him that I didn't want to let go of, or the fantasy of what I wanted our life to be like together?

I know… I know.

At this point, the woman he was living with—his girlfriend—his homegirl knew about our baby and the baby he'd had with the other woman, but she still didn't know about the newest pregnant woman

from the job. One day while talking, he casually mentioned that *she*—his girlfriend was also now pregnant.
"Oh I thought I told you" were his exact words

Of course she was. I mean it was only a matter of time.

He always said that she wanted a baby. Meanwhile, he was still telling me how much he loved me and wasn't going to let me go and didn't want me to give up on him. He reassured me he was working hard to make things better, and in spite of it all, there I was still holding on to the fucking hope.
He was always a man of convenience.
That woman, his girlfriend, was now his home.
He had me and our new normal, and the other women. He was winning.
But "us" started to feel like something dirty, something ugly. The deeper he got with his girlfriend, the further away I felt from him. He was distant and more unavailable than usual.

One day I found myself beginning to ask him if this is what he thought I deserved, but before the words could escape my throat, I realized it was actually what *I thought* I deserved.
The reality of me not knowing my own worth was becoming harder and harder to run from.

He didn't understand why I was pulling back and why would he? He had already gotten accustomed to how things were, and his theory was, "We have a good thing going here, why mess it up? You were okay with it when I had a wife so what's the problem now?"

It wasn't just the words that hurt, it was that I gave him all the liberty to say them to me.
What comeback would I have for that?
He was right.
He had a wife and I stayed.
He left his wife for his girlfriend, and I stayed.
He got another woman pregnant, and I stayed.
He got another woman after that pregnant and I stayed.
So now that his girlfriend was pregnant, why was I making that an issue?
I thought about all the things that they would share together that I never got to share with him, and it not only made me feel so sad but also discouraged, *done.*
I was over it…the cycle…the insanity.
Maybe not over him just yet but definitely over the situation and being in it.
How did I do this to myself?
Why did I do this to myself?
To my son…

Someone once said to me that I was smarter than my situation and those words couldn't ring truer. As if all the other things weren't enough, I was extremely disappointed in myself.

Talk is cheap

Sometimes we need to close our ears and open our eyes.

The biggest lesson I should have learned from him right from the beginning was *talk is cheap*.
I didn't judge him for all that he was doing, I just felt sorry for him. Granted he was doing it to himself, but I didn't understand why, and it still was hard to watch. He looked so lost and miserable half the time.

I know that he felt like he was losing his grip on me because my birthday was coming up and he decided to plan something for us to reconnect and figure everything out that we needed to figure out.

At first, I didn't really see any point to it but I'd be lying if I said that a small part of me wasn't happy that he was making an effort. It felt like I mattered, like we mattered, and he wanted to save us. His favorite words to me were "I'll take care of you"
"Don't give up on me"
and my all-time favorite (pun intended) "Time will tell".
I'd often ask him what time could possibly tell me that he hadn't already shown me.
We had our getaway. We did a lot of fun things, went out, partied, lounged at the beach and

poolside, restaurants, the gun range and even a strip club. We tried to have deep seeded conversations sitting on our balcony while enjoying our spectacular view, but it was always interrupted by the lust. There was immense passion. I don't think we ever had each other as much as we did in those few days. The fun was great, but we didn't accomplish anything other than prove that we could have amazing sex at an expensive resort. He wasn't really present except for those moments.

He was busy on his phone most of the time either taking care of business or pacifying his girlfriend. I mean, I couldn't blame him, what excuse would he possibly have for not checking in on his pregnant woman? I wasn't mad, I completely understood. The icing on the cake was when it was time to leave. He ended up staying behind to take care of more business, so I was left to travel back home alone. What else was new, though? That was our relationship—me being alone.

I figured out where I stood with him, accepted my position, and made the effort to just fall back, but he wouldn't just let me be. He claimed to love me, but I was always left wondering how. When I look back on things now, I'm able to see that it had been me all along. I was constantly chasing and begging for time with him, and the minute I stopped doing that everything changed. I told him I had no problem just being one of his baby's mother, but he insisted that I would always be more. He insisted that he loved me and wasn't letting me go, but the truth was he just wanted to live his life and save me as a back-up plan. I told him if he really did love me, then he would leave me alone.

Every promise that he ever made to me were empty ones, pacifiers to keep me quiet and make me think that everything would be alright. It worked for a long time because a part of me was always holding on to the hope that maybe, just maybe, one day we would get our time. But the years were just going by and there I was still waiting, hoping and wishing. If that wasn't some real-life, low vibrational shit, I don't know what is.

He has spread himself so thin that he would never be able to give me what I truly wanted or deserved. I've never been the type to half ass anything, so why was I doing it now? Why was I accepting the crumbs that he had been giving me? The entire situation no longer sat right within my spirit. Now that I had a child with him, I had no choice but to deal with him, but definitely not in the ways I had been.

His life seemed to be coming together, all of his hopes and dreams were coming through and that was a good thing. I always believed in him and wished him all the best, but his life was with someone else.

I had to accept us for what we were and not what I wanted us to be.

The shift

"As you are shifting, you will begin to realize that you are not the same person you used to be. The things you used to tolerate have become intolerable. Where you once remained quiet, you are now speaking your truth. Where you once battled and argued, you are now choosing to remain silent. You are beginning to understand the value of your voice and there are some situations that no longer deserve your time, energy, and focus." – Anonymous

This is the moment where I had to ask myself some tough questions and answer them honestly.
If the answers didn't give me clarity, then I wasn't being honest with myself. Nothing changes if nothing changes, so when he said things such as "You're not going anywhere," and "You were okay with everything when I had a wife," he was right.

I accepted his low efforts.
I never said no to him.
I was always available to him.
I was always at his beck and call.
I always gave into him.
I never stayed mad at him.

He took full advantage of it all, and why wouldn't he? He was already a selfish person who evidently didn't care too much about his own life, so why would I expect him to care about mine? They say we teach people how to treat us…I sure as hell taught him how to treat me, didn't I?

The nerve of me always speaking about his words not matching his actions, when in fact, my actions didn't match the things I said I wanted for myself, either. Everything in life is a choice, and once I truly came to terms with this and began licking my own wounds of denial, delusion, embarrassment, and self-betrayal, I stopped worrying about what he was or wasn't doing and started paying more attention to what *I* was doing.
Rather than focusing on the way I felt about him, I began facing the hard facts of the situation I had put myself in, and that was hard. To see that he was what I kept choosing for myself over and over again was really, really hard.
Taking accountability for ourselves isn't easy, which is why so many of us would rather run from it. I hated that this was the man that I wanted.
I hated having to watch him live his life with someone else.
I hated how I felt when he left.
I hated being in the situation, but I had to stop feeling sorry for myself because I was the one who put myself there.

I had to stop getting caught up in the empty promises and the breadcrumbs. I made the conscious decision to be with a married man so what did I really think would happen? I had to adjust my thinking, shift my focus, and change my mindset.

I had to unpack, peel back all of my layers and look deep within. Journaling was a game changer for me, it helped to alleviate my chronic overthinking, and allowed me to face myself and my situation for what it truly was. *It birthed this book.*

I researched, got resources, followed positive women on Instagram who had been in my shoes before and listened to them. I started reading more and learned about things like shadow work and mirror work. I also got my ass into therapy which was extremely important. I genuinely wanted and needed to figure out more about myself, and why—knowing how *not* good he was for me—I held onto to him for so long.

Of course, nothing happened overnight. Admittedly, while I was intentionally putting in the work, I still wasn't implementing all of the things I was learning one hundred percent. He'd come around and I'd still follow him down the rabbit hole, and like a bad hangover, I would pay for it the next day.

The thing about him that I always felt was so hard to explain was this: he wasn't a bad person.

Yes, he was selfish, a player, community dick...but he never once raised his voice at me, raised a hand

to me, called me out of my name, or spoke down to me, and that meant everything to me.
In my relationships before him, I experienced all of those things. So even though he wasn't what a knight in shining armour would look like to everyone else, when you've been in those kinds of toxic relationships, someone like him coming around and treating you well while in your presence (regardless of what he was doing outside of the time you spent together) was *my* knight in shining armour.

This is why healing is so important.
This is why learning what your worth it is so important.
This is why inner work, self-reflection, and self-honesty is so important.
Until you fix whatever is broken inside of you, you will always choose men who give you just a *little* bit better than the last, hence why we accept and yearn for the breadcrumbs. I realized that I was operating from my lower vibrational self—desperate, self-sabotaging, toxic, codependent, with a crippling fear of abandonment. It became crystal clear that if I ever wanted to meet and step into the version of myself who vibrates higher, then I would have to take the initiative to heal myself.

It was time to grow up.

It was time to take accountability for myself, my life, and my decisions.

What's lower than rock bottom?

August 2021 that's what.

It's always when we decide that we're really done with someone and actually taking the strides away from them that some bullshit happens, isn't it?
My period was late. I laughed to myself thinking, "Nah… There's no way..."
I took a home pregnancy test just to be sure.
The test was positive.
I didn't tell him right away because I needed to process it first. I was so angry at myself. Here I was pregnant once again for this man who I knew I needed to get away from.

The next day during his lunch break, he called me and could sense that something was up by the way I was speaking.
"Are you okay?" He asked.
I didn't bother to beat around the bush.
"I'm pregnant," I replied, flatly.
I didn't expect him to jump for joy, but I also didn't expect the reaction that I got either. His words that day will forever be imprinted on my brain...*on my heart*
"I have enough kids, and I don't want any more of them. If you decide to keep this baby, it'll be all on

you. I'll only deal with the son we already have together. You'll have to take care of this child on your own."

What?

Tears started pouring down my face, much like they are right now as I'm writing this, but as usual, I didn't say much. I just listened to him continue listing the reasons why he didn't want any more kids. When I felt like he was done, I thanked him for being honest and ended the conversation. About a week later, he came by so we could talk more about it. This time there was less venom, but the same message. He said that he wished he could tell me to bring the child to term but he had so much on his plate.

The following week I booked an appointment for an abortion. I sent him a text about it, but he never responded.

The following days after that were really rough. I was starting to get morning sickness. I didn't want to get out of bed, I was barely eating and all I could find the energy to do was cry. Based on my calculations, I was already about six weeks along, and I was consumed by guilt. I cried so much that I gave myself headaches. One day, in the midst of one of my crying fits, I got a text reminder about my upcoming appointment for the abortion, and it sent me straight over the edge.

I wanted to run away. I wished I could just take my kids, pack up, and move to a place far, far away. I would have my baby without having to worry about anybody else. My eyes were red, puffy, and burning. The new tears stung my face. Moments later I got a random text from him saying that his other baby had been born.

"Congratulations," I responded. What else was I supposed to say? Once again, I was alone, and telling him how I felt was pointless. All I could do was talk to God and ask Him my favorite question, "How did I get myself here?"

Definitely a rhetorical question but I wasn't happy with myself. I was disappointed, disgusted and ashamed because I was reckless yet again.

Now here I was at a crossroads making the biggest decision of my life. I had already made up my mind and he definitely had already made up his mind. It's like I had no choice but then again everything is a choice...right? I had no help, and I didn't have his support. God never gives us more than we can handle, right? Yes, that's true, but here I was a single mom of five, my son had just turned one. Would I be able to give this baby a proper life? I would definitely give it love, but could my love make up for the love of a father who didn't want it? I felt so lost, confused, and helpless. I didn't know what to do. I was losing my mind and the time was just drawing nearer.

On the day of the appointment, I woke up with a heavy heart, got myself ready, and made my way to the doctors office. When I got there, after giving my info to the front desk receptionist, I looked around as I found a chair to sit in. There were four other women of different ages and ethnic backgrounds, sitting and waiting, who all shared one thing in common. I was nervous and anxious. I didn't want to be there. I wanted to be at home in bed cuddled up with my baby like we do every other Saturday. I felt the tears welling up in my eyes, but fought them back. I heard the nurse call a woman's name and knew it was only a matter of time before she called mine.

"Annata?" she finally called.

She led me back to a room where she asked me to lower my pants below my stomach so she could do an ultrasound. I followed instructions and laid back as she put the cold gel on my stomach and repeated 75% percent of the questions that I was asked at the front desk. Then she asked, "Do you want to see the baby?"

After seeing my reaction, she explained that she was required to ask. Reluctantly, I agreed, and she turned the screen toward me. She asked if I would like a picture, also a required question, and I agreed to that as well. After the examination I cleaned up and was instructed to go back to the waiting area.

I sat there and all I could see was my baby in my head. Moments later another woman called me and escorted me to another office. More questions but this time she took my vitals and explained what was going to happen next. I had opted for the abortion pill. She explained how it worked and gave instructions on how I had to take it. At that point, I was a shell of a person. Just a body sitting in a chair in a cold office.

After she was finished and handed me all of the paperwork, including my picture, she told me to sit again in the waiting area and the doctor would call me. It was all starting to feel so final as if I was about to walk the plank.
I called my sister and she immediately sensed that something was up. As we were talking, I switched the call to video and turned the camera to the paperwork in my hand. Her mouth stood open as she saw it. She was shocked and at a loss for words.
"Are you okay?" she finally managed.
"No, I'm not," I answered.

Before we could continue our conversation, I heard my name called for a third time.
"I'm going to call you when I'm done," I told her.

I followed behind the elderly lady as she led me to yet another room which was similar to the first in that it also had an examination table.
I sat in the chair across from her and we looked at each other in silence for what felt like an eternity, but was probably only thirty seconds.

"Are you ready?" She finally asked.

The tears started streaming down my face.
"I don't know..." was all I could manage to get out of my mouth.
I wasn't ready. I'd never be ready.
The doctor suggested that I take a little more time to think about my decision because she knew firsthand how difficult it could be. She also advised that I talk with the on-site counselor. I'd already spoken in depth to my own therapist but she was right when she said "It always helps to have people to talk to." I felt like I was suffocating, keeping a dirty little secret, so I met with the counselor and we both felt like it was a good idea to take some more time to decide. I left the office feeling a lot more relieved than I did going in. I ended up taking the bus straight to my mother's house because sometimes all you really need is your mom.

That night he texted me to ask if I was okay and if I wanted to talk about it. I was shocked that he even remembered. I told him I wasn't and that I didn't go through with it. I got his favorite response…

Sigh.

Perspective

8/30/21

No problem can be solved from the same level of consciousness that created it - Einstein

The naive part of me wanted him to be happy because of the "love" I thought we shared. Instead, everything felt so *impersonal.*

I took a minute and got brutally honest with myself, looking at things from a different perspective.
Had I gotten pregnant by a random man would my decision be so difficult, or would it be obvious? Would it? There was no doubt in my mind that I wouldn't have the baby. So did I want to keep the baby just because it was with him? I wouldn't be the first woman who kept a baby because of a man, but I couldn't do it. He already made it clear how he felt. I couldn't do that to myself, *I couldn't do that to my baby.*
Nothing magical would have happened.

This was the best decision for everyone.

Until we meet again

My Sweet Baby,

Please forgive me.
It breaks my heart that you will never get to see this world because of me and my circumstances.
I'm sorry.

This has been the toughest decision of my life because I never imagined I'd be here doing this. I know that love is definitely not something that you would have lacked, I'm just not in a position to give you the life that you deserve. I'm barely making it. My time and resources are so limited, and I don't ever want to have to deprive any of you of anything. I had to say goodbye to you, and it was so hard. I love you so much and thank you for strengthening me.

Love Always

Your Mom.

Numb

It doesn't ever get easier, you just get stronger. I know that God forgives me. I just had to work on forgiving myself.

It had been almost two weeks since I had the abortion. We weren't in communication at all at that point when I got a random text.

"Hey, how are you?
"I'm good."
"How's the baby?"
"There is no more baby. I had the abortion almost two weeks ago."
"WHAT THE FUCK? Why?"
"What do you mean why? You said what you said, and you were right. Another baby wouldn't have been a good idea for either one of us."
"I just needed time to think, why didn't you just give me time."
"What time? You never asked for time. You simply listed your many reasons why this wasn't something you wanted. You even said that you wish you could tell me to bring it to term but you can't."
"I was in a dark place, and the more I thought about it the more the baby would have pushed me to work even harder. I just needed time. Why didn't you tell me?"

"The night before my appointment I called you. You didn't answer and you never called me back."
"Fuck. Fuck. Fuck."

That was the end of that.

Two days later he called me to say he had to make a run somewhere and he was on his way to pick me up so that I could ride with him, and we could talk. I wanted to say no and that there was nothing more to talk about, but I just didn't have the energy to go back and forth so I simply agreed.
The car ride was silent at first. He purposely played song after song that he knew represented something to us. Songs that we've played and sent to each other in the past. I looked out the window at the city lights and just listened. Finally, he decided to break the silence, "I'm sorry I hurt you."

I didn't respond.

I appreciated his apology though, because it wasn't something that he ever really did. He never admitted fault in anything that he did and would always make excuses and maintain his arrogant stance. To hear an apology as simple as it was felt sincere. It just goes to show how I was still in the pattern of putting his words on a pedestal.

When we stopped, I stayed in the car while he took care of what he had to do. When he returned to the car, he opened my door, gently cupped his hands around my face and kissed me softly. No hunger, just humility.

When we got back to my house, he shut the car off, opened my door, took my hand and led me out. We went upstairs where he took me in his arms, and I broke down in a fit of tears.

I felt so broken by the very man whose arms I was in, holding me as if holding me together.

He wiped my tears and said that crying was never something he ever wanted to see me do because of him. There was irony in that statement because all I did was cry due to him, but he had just never seen me do it in front of him.

He kissed my forehead, then my eyes, then my cheeks and then my lips…then we had sex.

After we just laid there, my head on his chest, his hands in my hair like any other regular night.

"I want my baby back," he whispered. I never responded because I knew in my soul that it was something that would never happen again.

The next morning before I went to work, I stopped in the 24HR Rite Aid and purchased a Plan B.

Relapse

I remember once he mistakenly mentioned to me about the time that I compared him to medicine. I immediately checked him and told him he had the wrong chick because I would never compare him to medicine. From the very beginning I always described him as DRUGS.

Medicine heals, drugs numb. Medicine is consistent, drugs are temporary. Drugs make you feel good in the moment, but then it's back to reality of chasing another high. He wasn't just a high, he was the ultimate high and my real addiction. Sometimes I felt like a part of me would always belong to him and he knew it. It didn't matter who came before him or who may come after him, it would always be him.
To this day I can't bring myself to stay angry at him no matter what he has done, and no matter how upset I was at him. I tried. I really tried.

God always shows us what we need to see, then He sits back and waits to see what we do with what He's shown us. If we do the right thing, then we get the blessings in the lesson. If we do the wrong thing, then it's back to the drawing board.
I had the abortion thinking that it would definitely be the end of us and the end of me holding on to

something that didn't exist. I thought it was the straw that broke the camel's back.
I told myself that I would use it as fuel to be stronger and to do better.

It's time...

Healing for real this time

Healing is a process that cannot begin if you keep holding on to what is hurting you.

Holding on doesn't stop the process, but it definitely delays it.

I kept sleeping with him not because he was so irresistible, but because I had a weakness within myself. Clearly something that I needed to work on. It was the only time I felt seen, heard or connected to him. I felt like I was healing as I was dealing with him, which I'm aware sounds like the oxymoron of the century. Of course you can't heal in the same environment where you became sick. But I naively felt that as time went by and I became more aware and started owning my shit, that I was getting stronger. My entire mindset began to shift and change, and it felt good.

I am far from being a failure, but my lack of discipline landed me in situations that I didn't need to be in. The awareness and accountability was the shift that I needed. Owning my poor decisions. Healing isn't pretty; it's hard, messy, lonely and it doesn't happen overnight, but it's necessary and it's your responsibility. Healing isn't about being perfect, it's about getting to know yourself and loving yourself the way you want others to love

you. People are mirrors in your life to show you exactly what you're doing to yourself. We love to call people toxic when in fact we are being toxic to ourselves by the choices that we make.
To a certain degree, every relationship requires some sort of compromise, but I've learned that if the compromise will cost me my dignity, self-respect, self-worth, integrity and morals then it's not the relationship for me.

I remember him once saying to me that whoever was with him had to accept that they would only get fifty percent of him, because the other fifty percent was for other things. It was a sad day when I admitted to myself that not only was I willing to accept less than even fifty.
Let's call it what it was: I was *desperate* and settling for whatever I could get.
He could only offer what he had to offer, and he spread himself so thin that there was nothing to really offer. I never blamed him though I mean how could I when I knowingly and willingly kept choosing to further entangle myself deeper.
We love these men hard, accept them for who they are, fuck them like there's no tomorrow, give them everything they want and be there for them in any way they need but it won't stop them from doing whatever they want to do. So we have to do what's best for us.

So many of us women go through life seeking closure from a man, when the closure is always right in front of our faces, within ourselves.
I'm still not all the way healed from this situation, but I am navigating as best as I can. I'm no longer broken the way I once was, and that's progress. I realized through this that no man ever loved me the way that I wanted or needed to be loved because I didn't love myself the way I was supposed to *first*.

Annata 2.0

Who am I now?

I'm not perfect, but I'm dope in real life, and I no longer shy away from saying that out loud.
I definitely have insecurities, but I own everything about myself—the good, bad, ugly, the beautiful and everything else in between. It doesn't matter what I've been through, I will never be jaded, and I am unapologetic about that. My past doesn't define me and it doesn't dictate my present or my future. Nobody can tell me about myself because I know me better than anybody else. Accountability has set me free in so many ways. I feel like a brand-new woman with as new lease on life. I don't preach and I don't judge because I understand that everyone has their own path to take.
I know my strengths, my weaknesses, my flaws, and my triggers. I know my heart and my soul.

I know who I am *now*.
I may have kissed a few frogs and taken some wrong turns on this love journey, but that's okay because it's all a part of the process.
Everything happens for a reason, and everything thus far has led me to the transformation I so desperately needed. Learning self-love has shown me that my forever love is me.

Onto the next chapter...

Do you believe in magic?

They say you mustn't do permanent things with temporary people...guess I got that memo a little too late.

People always tell me that I have my head in the clouds and that I live in a fantasy world. I never think anything of it because I do believe in magic, I one hundred percent believe in love...*real love.* I believe in love simply because of the way that I love. *I always* love hard, deep and free because in my book that's the only way to love. I am never ashamed to admit it. When I love you, you definitely feel it.

It wasn't until recently that I decided to change my narrative. I no longer identified as being a hopeless romantic, a *hopeful* romantic had a much better tone. All that I've been through—the failed relationships, my marriage ending, and loving someone who didn't really love me—I still haven't given up. I know that love will happen when the time is right. A wonderful man will enter my life and he won't be like the others.
How do I know?
Because I'm no longer the version of myself who accepted the others.

My therapist asked me once what my perfect guy would look like if I had a magic wand, and initially I wants to use my magic wand to give him his freedom. Sigh I had to get myself to a place where I'd use my magic wand for myself and as simple as it sounds, my perfect guy would be a man who appreciates me wholeheartedly, respect me continuously and love me unconditionally. My every effort and every quirk. He'd love me at my best and love me even more at my worst.
Sounds magical right? Yes a dream come true.
My magic wand would be me meeting my forever love...my person. The one whose type of love I can also feel.

"Type" love

The type of love that I want is the...
"Have you seen the way he looks at her" type love.
That can't keep our hands off each other in the elevator type love.
That "Come outside, I bought you lunch" type love.
That "I saw this and thought about you" type love.
That PDA type love.
That "Let's see what we can do in the ten minutes before we check out" type love.
That "Let's go to church" type love.
That "Kiss me in the rain" type love.
That "Let's have a picnic in the park" type love.
That "Babe, I ran a bath for you" type love.
That "Let's go for a walk on the beach in time to catch the sunset" type love.
That hand on my thigh while we're driving type love.
That red light kisses type love.
That "Let's get matching tattoos" type love.
That "Baby get dressed, I'll pick you up at eight" type love.
That road trip type love.
That "Let me come over just to lay next to you" type love.
That "Pack your bags, I planned a nice weekend for us" type love.

That dance parties in the kitchen while we're cooking dinner type love.
That "Let's take a break and spend the day doing nothing together" type love.
That "I have this business idea we can do together," type love.
That never go to bed angry type love.
That "Babe I took your car to get it serviced" type love.
That "I'm so glad you're mine" type love.
That Sunday type love.

I want the type of love that lasts a *lifetime*.

Release

I surrender.

Loving you was always a losing game that I chose to keep playing. No regrets, just lessons learned.

I realize that I've been too caught up and way too focused on the wrong things, namely you. I've been asking questions that you can't answer. Wanting things from you that you can't provide. Expecting things from you that you can't deliver. The truth is it's not even on you though, it's on ME.

We love each other. We have amazing chemistry and an undeniable connection. You always say that it's in the kiss and it really is in the kiss. When we kiss a fire ignites inside us both and just stays burning. That passion is so real, so rare, so powerful, so beautiful and I love it, but it doesn't mean that we're aligned.

We're on separate paths right now and that's actually a good thing. But by me holding on to you, it's like I'm trying to go down your path and forsaking my own. Holding on would mean wanting you to be something that you can't be. Holding on would mean continuing to hurt myself knowing the reality of the situation. As much as I don't talk about it, my position in this situation hurts. It hurts to see you with someone else. It hurts to hear how wonderful she is. It hurts to feel like a dirty little secret. It hurts that you're there for her in so many ways that you've never been for me. It all just hurts. I'm not saying that you hurt me intentionally, I'm just saying that whether or not I like to admit it these things do hurt. Holding on would mean me further choosing to play with my karma, because I'd be making the decision to continue to be the other woman knowing that you have a woman that you share your life with who is good to you. How can I expect you to care about my karma when you don't even care about your own? You talked about the part in your journey that she plays and the part that your wife played, but what part do I play? You always say that you have to make some wicked sacrifices. Unfortunately, I get to be the wickedest one. You ask me to give you time and not to give up on you, and I did my best to be understanding and patient with you, to work with you. I loved you so much and so freely that I never once tried to possess you, but in the end none of it mattered because it still wasn't enough. The one thing stronger than chemistry, connection, and passion is free will… and you exercised yours.

She is your home, and I am your adventure—I get it. Home will always come before adventure. What you don't understand about me is that I am a home AND an adventure in one, unfortunately just not for you. I can't force you to see that I am a blessing, but the truth is you already know that I am. But you have so many blessings to choose from that everyone gets lost in the shuffle. We've all been trying to do things to stand out and show you what value we bring to the table, but I have nothing to prove anymore. You said it yourself that I am a good woman and I'll probably find a man, but it might not be real. The truth is, though, wherever I go or whoever I end up with it will be real because I AM REAL—always been, and always will be, and that's why you love me the way you do. I get you, I see you, I genuinely accept and understand you for who you are without judging you or trying to change you, but it doesn't matter because once again you made your choice, and it wasn't me. They say to choose people who choose you.

I've finally chosen me.

Where do we go from here?

Your last mistake will be your greatest teacher.

Sometimes you want a relationship to work out so badly that you are willing to sacrifice so much for it.
Why?
So that people can complement you on how lovely you look together? Or fifty years down the line you can say that you made it?
Sure, you made it, but at what cost?
Is it real if it's forced? Is it real if it's dysfunctional? Is it worth it? Worth what exactly?
People measure love by many different things such as how much you do for them, how much you can endure with them, etc. However, love isn't something that can be measured. *Unconditional love cannot be measured.*

Unconditional love though, isn't the same as unconditional tolerance and I say that just to say I do forgive my baby daddy but more so I forgive myself. I can't change what has happened, but I discovered in one of my therapy sessions that everything changed for me when I no longer made him my priority.
My well-being is now my priority.

Our newest normal has to be co-parenting peacefully—nothing more—it's the best thing we can do for our son. However, I realize that it's up to me to enforce that boundary, then be loyal to it.

My Story

My story is just that…*my story.*
It's not meant to bash him or expose him. It has served as a bonus tool in my healing journey.
Letting it out and making it real.
Some will read my words and wonder why I stayed. Others will be able to relate and understand exactly why I stayed because it's probably why they also stayed.

Was he a poor choice? Without a doubt.
Do I regret him? Never.
Did I learn a lesson? I learned a lot of lessons.

When I finally closed my ears and opened my eyes.
I learned.

Experience will always be your greatest teacher and we all have our own lives to live but I do encourage you to learn from me because it is said that a smart person learns from his own mistakes, but a wise person learns from other people's mistakes.

From me to You

It's important for you to understand that love is a beautiful thing, and you deserve it. We face many challenges in life as is, love shouldn't have to be one of them. Struggle-love should never be a thing. I know you've heard it many times before, and as cliche as it sounds—*self-love* really is the right answer to every question.

I am no expert, but I've been a girlfriend, a wife, a side chick, and a side chick to a side chick, so I speak from experience.

Self-love is the master key that unlocks all of the other doors to love.

Real love.
Healthy love.
Unconditional love.
Forever love.

If we don't love ourselves properly, how do we plan on loving others properly? We have to set the tone, and if nothing else, I hope my story proved to you that much.

UN APOLOGETICALLY UNJADED
what loving him taught me about myself

www.ingramcontent.com/pod-product-compliance
Lightning Source LLC
Chambersburg PA
CBHW032019040426
42448CB00006B/663